About the Author

Writer. Empath. Lover.

Brown Skin Bruises

K.W.

Brown Skin Bruises

Olympia Publishers
London

www.olympiapublishers.com
OLYMPIA PAPERBACK EDITION

A CIP catalogue record for this title is
available from the British Library.

ISBN: 978-1-80439-502-8

This is a work of fiction.
Names, characters, places and incidents originate from the writer's
imagination. Any resemblance to actual persons, living or dead, is
purely coincidental.

First Published in 2023

Olympia Publishers
Tallis House
2 Tallis Street
London
EC4Y 0AB

Printed in Great Britain

Acknowledgements

Thank you for the help and inspiration. You know who you are.

Preface

I never considered myself a poet. I honestly still don't. I thought those small lines that I occasionally jotted down, which exposed every part of me, were just entries in a diary. I didn't think I had enough depth to seep into others' thoughts with my words. The beauty of me being wrong in this situation is that I can share my own piece of art with the world.

I hope that this work is able to spark discussions about mental health within the black community. We, in all our sun-kissed glory, believe that our beautiful brown skin cannot bruise. From day one we have been taught that sticks and stones can break our bones, but words can never hurt us. This was wholly true when it was happening to our ancestors every day. We have to be strong, show no weakness. Individuals as part of the black community are told that their mental health struggles simply are not real or could simply be fixed by taking a nap or praying it away. I want to be a person that can help my people see that needing help for a pain you cannot physically see or feel does not make you weak and that it is indeed still pain. I wish to share my experience living in that world, dealing with those traumas, and how I try to overcome it.

I have to admit, this process, and future release to others, fills me with anxiety. What if no one likes it? What if people judge me? What if I'm looked at differently? Eventually, I just had to realize that this is genuine, it's real, it's me and that the perception of me that everyone may gain isn't valid. With every piece I produce I aim to be completely honest and to make a difference. I aim to express myself over it all.

I cried, celebrated, laughed, got angry, and even got anxious several times during this process, but at the end of the day I believe I will be presenting something that I'm proud of. I hope I am able to educate others on how black mental health looks and how to grow from those not so good days. I can say that this pain is worth it.

The Trauma.

The heartbreak, the bullying, the sexual assault. It all became too much. Everyone was leaving their mark without me even knowing it. I avoided memories that lived in my favorite places, and I let everything make me forget who I am. I let myself forget who I was. That's the funny thing about trauma. It wants to control you. It wants to become not only a part of you, but to consume you. Escaping the thoughts seemed impossible unless I was writing. Poetry became an escape I never thought of. It helped me learn that trauma is not a fan of expression.

I let things from my past impact my present and every day became hard to live through. Not only were the thoughts getting to me, but I thought I had no one to lean on, no one to call a friend. It was an extremely lonely time. It gave me a lot of time to learn who I was. It got to a point that I was finally able to transfer my feelings to paper again. I started using my poetry as a way to either reach out for help or to simply explain how I'm feeling since there was no other way that I could. Not until later did I realize there was a message in each pen stroke and my journals were quivering waiting to explode and be released.

I still feel most of these things and sometimes I can't shake it. That is what trauma does. It's a dark cave. It's the bottom of an empty, wet well. It's a plane falling out of the sky; it's scary and it feels hopeless, but that doesn't mean it is. It's time to proudly wear the scars from the vulnerability.

Me

I am not a poet.
I use these words to shine
A light on the darkness inside.
Every comma, every rhyme
Breaks at the place where I hide.

Every mistake, every wound,
It all reminds me that I will
Forever be doomed,
No darkness nor hiding
Can ever stop the pain from rising

Up, up my throat,
So much bile and sick
It makes me think I'll choke.

I wish I was better with my words.
I wish my spirit was kinder to my thoughts.

I wish they were nicer to my body.

My heart has always been my downfall.
I scream words to ears that do not hear.
I expose my spirit to hearts that do not beat.
And I move my body for eyes that only crave me for one night.

Frustration

Even when things just start
I get grasped by the heart.
I'm putting all my feelings on the line,
Please don't waste my time.

I'm all the way out there
Floating on the wings of every girl's prayer,
Wanting the pain to cease,
Knowing I'm the only one who can provide my own peace.

My feelings are just a page in your black book,
You're having fun knowing you've got me on the hook.
I'm a person, not a game.
I don't even need you to feel the same.
Just don't bring me into this.

I choose to hate the player and the game.
Even myself for thinking a nigga was gonna change.

I'm too tired of this shit.
I just need to relieve this frustration.

I said "Goodbye" to us yesterday.
Today I told myself it was the last time.

I have grown tired
Of the punches you throw with your words.
They leave me bruised and battered for days,
Months,
Years.

I can still see the black eye you gave me
From when you said I had no respect for myself.
My arm is still broken
From when you cheated several times.

This bump on my head is new though.
It's from hitting my head
When you made it clear that all I'd ever be
Was someone you called on in need.

She's selfish,
She's loud,
She doesn't like disagreements.

"Things always have to be her way."
She's mean,
She's unforgiving,

She's a bitch.
"There's always something depressing going on with her."
She's too sad.

Does anyone even know her?

You called her a nerd before you found out her name.
You judged her weight before you knew her age.

She's spiraling, she's tired
But she'll one day be free.

Baby "she" was always me.

How am I supposed to grow
If you won't let me?
I'm a sunflower getting
Cut for her seeds
And used to make nectar.

My petals have been picked
For "He loves me" or nots
But I ended on the sour note.
That's why you tossed me away?

I had no more to
Physically provide
So you stopped me from
Moving on and growing

So you can throw me aside.
It all makes sense now.
I was better off not knowing.

Long Term

I want you back in my life even though everyone tells me it
isn't right...

I talk to you, but you don't hear me.
I reach for you, but you act like you don't see.

You make me feel my heartbeat in my throat,
You make me reconsider everything that I ever wrote,
You control my thoughts even when you don't try.

You can have everything you want
Which I'm willing to be.
I just want you to want me
But one of us gotta be let down.
When I figured out it was me I began to cry,

I refuse to believe this is love
But what else makes a person
Take every painful breath?

What else makes a person
Wake up to start their day?

What fucking else
Could make it possible

For me not to forget you?

I'll continue this journey of
"Us" on my own
Because that's how I started it.
But at least my heart got
To feel your grasp
During the time.

The real me is
Stuck behind the mask
Screaming eternally.

Fit In

I'm not a bitch,
I don't do cliques,
I just want them to like me.

I'll talk on the phone,
I don't want to be alone.
Somebody save me.

You ostracize
Because you don't understand
Even when I'm trying
To hold out my hand

It's not enough for you.
I gotta
Be loose to be cool
But that's not what I wanna do.

People laugh and taunt
I wish I could say "so what?"
But I can't do it

Cause I just wanna fit.

I like my demons more than my real friends.
Maybe that's exactly why
I choose to spend all my time with them.

Unwanted

Blood boils when you touch me
But I don't like it.
You try to force me
But I fight it.

My mind wanders
To when I wasn't here,
When wasn't I here?

I can't seem to remember.

You keep losing your temper.
Maybe if I stare at the wall
I won't have to think about it at all.

I can't say "don't touch me"
Because I want you to love me.
This is the only way.
This is my fault.
I'm ashamed.

I never knew this
Temptation
Would lead to all the
Manipulation.

Ignoring the abuse
Because what's the use
Only waiting for it to get better.

I know I'm being stupid
And I blame it all on Cupid
Because what has become of me?
I'm not like what I see.

I just want to be happy and free.

Excitement and glee flee from my body
As I hear the tone of your voice,
The taste and the tint of
What you had to drink
Lingers longingly on both of our lips
After the harshest of kisses.

When I give it up
I'll never be able to say I miss this.
The people around me really start to think
Especially when I start saying
"Nah, I don't want a drink."

It was ruined for me.
No more late-night love sessions
Due to your deadly obsession.
My heart convulsions quickly turned to
Fear and revulsion.

I don't even listen to my own advice
And until I do, I'll never get it right.
I started ignoring all the red flags.
The bad temper. Infrequent hugs. Backhanded compliments.
I worked constantly just to not make him mad,
That's how I knew I had it bad.

Even now when everything is said and done
I still think of you and of the times that were fun.

Fooled me once,
You took that blame,
If you fool me twice
I'll take the shame.

You beat me mentally until I can't see.
Time is on my side
But I can't figure out how to say goodbye.

My heart trembles when you're near,
Your presence being ever so clear.

I want to get rid of you
But I don't know what to do.

Deep

My heart has experienced treason,
This man has me smiling,
Elated,
All for no reason.

It's soul souring,
Never boring,
Irreversibly mesmerized.
This wasn't even the goal,
I didn't need anything
To seal the hole.

Numbered kisses
Living on every wire of my mind,
Almost tricking me into thinking
That you could ever be mine.

Inescapable,
Unforgettable,
Only wishing for one more look,
One more touch,
One more hug,
Longing to be the one who makes you fall in love.

It's a path I shouldn't even venture on.

I would feel better if I knew
This relationship was on loan.

I believe in romance again.
It's got me revealing my heart with this pen.
I don't want to move too fast
Due to failures from my past.

Holding your hand with my heart
And your heart with my body,
Even a day is too much apart
And I can't give myself to anybody.

You wanted me stuck,
Now I'm the one out of luck.
I've never felt like this before,
I wish I could just even the score.

This is a connection that's
Dividing me into sections
And I want it all on my sleeve
Just for you to see.

But you aren't ready for this blessing from above.
You aren't ready for all my love.

Sad Love Song

What happened to the intimacy?
You know the kind
That didn't involve being in me.

We used to lie skin to skin
Bursting from emotions within.
The compliments don't flow anymore,
Now no words are said
To make my heart soar.

It's lonely
Being in love
Especially when you're the only one.

That obsession led up to no affection
And sadness turns you on more than I ever could.
I get treated like this
All while hoping for bliss,
But I know it'll never come.

I only blame myself now when I'm all alone.
It feels like a sad love song.

Playa No More

Full moon,
Full lips,
Distracted with my thoughts
And wanting to feel hands on my hips.

I'm too high for this.

I would call him but
I know he's with some other bitch.
How I feel is irrelevant.
I just need to vent.
Especially if I'll never get back
All that time spent.

All I have is time,
It's occupied thinking of someone that was never mine.
When will it stop?
When will my eyes stop being glued to a clock?

Maybe I should be alone,
Ignore everybody and stop answering the phone.
Would that be enough?
Would that make my heart strong
And make me a lil tough?

I don't know wassup
But I'm hanging the jersey up.
There's nothing left to gain
And I'm tired of being in pain.

I was the best in the game
But the broken heart won't let me stay the same.

Missing You

I replaced you
But my mind refused to forget you.
I feel you in every step
And reject you with every breath.

Fuck you.
Just for leaving me so low.

Not empty, but hollow,
Not alone, but lonely,
Not sad, but depressed.
I feel like a mess,

I want it all back
Even if now I'm convinced
It was all just an act.
I do it all for you.
I wish you were around to see
Or at least even knew.

Not no longer here
But disappeared,
Not gone but working on forgotten.
I never knew words could tell such pretty lies
And that sweet kisses could turn rotten.

All I do is think about you.
I wish from the bottom of my heart that wasn't true.

Obsessed

I don't write love letters.
I have to know your feelings
And not reveal mine
Because it makes me feel better.

I feel stuck and blind,
Wishing I could just leave the memories behind.
At times I feel so tired,
That connection between our souls
Constantly keeping me wired.

Reading in between the lines
Proves it all
But I'll always be too proud to admit when I fall.

I wouldn't trade anything for it though,
I've never met someone who always has my heart in my
throat.
I can't figure out why
Whatever it is it makes me never wanna say bye.

It feels like an obsession.

They are
Touching me and teasing me
But you're the one I want pleasing me,

Hands on my smooth skin,
Whole time I'm wishing it was you again.

I hear your voice in my mind
Saying you wish we had more time,
Now I'm stuck thinking
Every knock on the door
Every ring of the bell
Every car on the block
Is you.

You told me you loved me, is that true?
I wanna compensate for the lost time.
What do we do?

It's not lost on me that you try,
That's the only reason I don't cry,
But even then I sit and ask myself why
I'm out of my depth with this connection
So much it's become an obsession.

I just want to know I'm not the only one,
Falling in love alone is never fun.

So forgive me for forgetting,
For stopping myself from wishin',
For trying someone new.
It's just to convince myself
I don't want you.

The Illness

Depression is a disease that has patience. It feeds off of stress, heartbreak, and loss. It grows with you and adapts to who you are at that time. Then, it starts bringing its friends. It's a party. My other party goers are anxiety and PTSD.

It took me years to finally begin treatment for my mental illnesses, but by that time I felt as though it was too late. Everything felt like it had sunk in. I had convinced myself that I was just sick and there was nothing that I could do about it, but I was wrong. I convinced myself that something was just wrong with me and maybe I deserve to feel this unbearable pain every day. I was wrong about that too, but they don't let you see that until it really is too late. They, the illnesses, have followed me, dragged me by my hair, and have even grown and blossomed with me.

With words I express these tormenting thoughts and those inexplicable feelings. People are not their illnesses, but they are a part of you and it's important to accept it and grow with it before it's too late.

My inner queen is haunted by her inner demons.

Do Better

Some people like to think they know
What it's like to wake up suffering.
To have their biggest dream be them
Jumping off a cliff.
They joke about death and leaving the earth
But what if that is your only thought?

What is a person to do when they are eternally internally
screaming forever?

Most people wonder
Who can they run to when they need love
But who can I run to when I want to live?
No one is there then.
All my life I've been there for people
Who were never there for me.

It has taken me all these years to realize
That things aren't meant to be one sided.
They have someone to run to, why don't I?
Why do I have to pay mine?

It costs nothing to be a shoulder to cry on
And it costs even less to actually listen when you're being
cried on.

"That's fine," I tell myself. "One day they'll care about my shit too."
But one day never comes and I'm back to phase one.

I'm tired of being depressed and of that shit getting suppressed.

My consciousness can't disrupt my dreams,
My inebriation propels my thoughts,
My vices are making me believe them.

On these nights
I can't create.
What starts off as
My written word
Come out like a
Diary entry.

I love my words
But sometimes
They just won't stop
And I need them to.

I've never been quick with my tongue
Just smart with it.
I let my words soar around my brain
Until it's the right time to
Spit them out.

Sometimes those words
Don't see the day.
I freeze. I shake.
I stop breathing,
My words leave me.

In a silent, terrified space
My surroundings disappear,
I'm filled with immense fear.

I'm no longer me,
I'm just a ball of anxiety.

Free Sailing

Drowning,
Suffocating,
Only asking why,
No longer able
To keep my eye on the prize.

Falling,
Spiralling,
Head no longer in the clouds,
Reality is hitting now.

A scam,
A sham,
Something to take over my life,
Never knowing
What will be the trigger next time.

Childlike was my thought process,
Little and in love,
Infatuated with ideas
That will never be.

Life is a limited fantasy!
But I continuously get caught up in
The Seas,

So I float
With no time to mope
Because when I do
I'm here.

Fighting for my life
In this endless ocean.

Sometimes the loneliness
Tries to become my
Best friend.

I tell it "No"
But it keeps trying,
It will never end.

It follows me to school,
To parties,
Even in all my dreams

I have no clue what it means.

In this quest
To find myself,
Maybe I will be able
To fight my loneliness.

I'm tired of you
Controlling my thoughts.
I can't handle you
Overwhelming my spirit.

How can I be free from you?
I feel like
I'm running out of time.
What can I do?

I smoke away the thoughts
Under the moon.
It's illuminating my soul.

I am
Contemplating,
Wondering
Will my time ever come?

Will I find my happiness?

Changing

I constantly make the same mistakes
And end up falling flat on my face.
I feel the need for space.

Floating infinitely,
Not wanting to get close intimately,
I never want to get lost in you
Because then you'll have all of me
And won't know what to do.

I only want hot kisses on my skin,
Not to care about where they've been.
I wanna see a head between my thighs
And to not care when I say goodbye.

This ends with me telling myself lies.

Toxic fantasy actively lives within me,
Wanting, fighting, hoping to be free.
I have to be more careful with whom I let see.

If I'm not, it could be the death of me.

Starry Night

My constellation
Distant and beautiful,
Fruitful,
No words hold the thoughts,
The thoughts hold no weight,
Holding on to peace caught
And joy is no longer a question.

Euphoria,
Nirvana,
No longer on this plain,
Only dreams hold all the pain.

I don't remember
A single thing about her.

Some say her eyes glistened,
You never had to question
If she actually listens.

Others say her voice was strong,
Maybe even compare it to your favorite song.

She walked into the room,
Smile on her face,
But assuming she was happy was everyone's mistake.

We never got to meet.

Can you lose your purpose?
Forget everything that
Makes it worth it?

I'm tired.

I sleep,
Barely eat,
Definitely don't speak.

I'm getting bigger
Physically,

I'm constantly sick
Mentally.

I know feeling better
Is all up to me
But truly a little help
Is all I need.

I can't get it though.
I'll attempt to make it alone.

What am I supposed to do?
The day is over,
The people are gone,
The house is empty.

What am I supposed to do?
The thoughts are growing louder,
My body is as heavy as a stone
The blades are calling my name.

I know what I want to do,
I want to stop shaking,
For my breathing to calm down,
To stay alive.

But I don't deserve it.

So what am I supposed to do?

Live Forever

I fear that resistance
That grows with persistence,
Of the inevitable end.

Times twisting,
Scared to be the one to feel death kissing.
No more wishing.
Only do.

If I let time pass me by
Then I'm a fool,
My own eloquence misused
Due to that substance abused,

Just to escape to the infinity
To which I've gained an affinity.
I'm trying to not look back
Because who likes living in the past?

Only focused on the road ahead of me,
Giving my life as pay,
Unable to seize the day.

I want to live forever.

Glass half empty,
I'll never make it.
I try to be positive
But I can't fake it.

Glass half empty,
I'm in a dark hole,
I'll do whatever it takes
To save my soul.

I viewed my glasses as
Half empty
To hide the fact that
They were never full at all.

If I keep going down this path
I'm going to fall.

Moving on

I'm better off secluded
And not included,
I like to think,
Then maybe wash it away with a drink.

People try to debate it
But it leaves me frustrated.
Is there something wrong with me?
There must be.

Friends and lovers alike,
They don't even think twice
When it comes to leaving me behind.

I'm the common denominator
And I want to know what's on their minds,
Like,
Is it easy to deceive me?
Why take a piece of my heart just to leave me?

I have a lot of questions
Especially after you've left all these impressions.

But I rather leave it where it is
Instead of wondering "What if...?"

I'm done with it all.
Not even available for a phone call.

Contemplating while
Shaking my head.
Drunk at a party,
Wishing I was in my bed.

I'm stuck
Trying to get home instead.
My thoughts are overwhelming,
My skin feels like it's melting.

This anxiety is getting the best of me.

Broken,
Frozen,
Abused,
Confused.

No matter what I do
I always lose.
I'm trying to handle this disease with ease
But it's winning.

I'm not worried about sinning,
There's no saving my soul
So don't make that your goal.

The darkness lives here
And we're friends,
I don't expect that to change again.

It's in the dead eye stare
And the sadness in the air.
It's in the up all nights
And the getting into fights.

Tear-stained pillowcases and
Unrecognizable faces,
Wanting to call on a friend
But the ties have all met their end.

Sick with realizations,
Feverish with no motivation,
Can I make the pain stop as a consolation?

Staring at the constellations,
Their secrets hide my joy
So I spend all night studying them,
Deciding I want to break hearts on a whim.

What a destructive path I'm on.
Is this all due to love scorn?

Me and my rage are never on the same page
Where I have a lover's heart
And she convinces me that I'm not even worth it
And it tears me apart.

Maybe I should be glad
That my illness is driving me mad.

End of Sad Girl Era

Flowers used to bloom in my heart
And my vision was rose colored,

Now I forget to water them
And I keep my eyes covered.

I'd rather feed the hunger
Than sit and wonder
When all it did was get me hurt.

What was it all worth?

I didn't listen to my own advice,
Now I come off too nice,

Now it's a world of seduction
With no heart since it's in construction.

To think this is all I thought I was good for,
Now it's the thrill that I live for.

The Learning

It takes maturity, peace within yourself, and love to heal and learn from past experiences and mistakes. It doesn't matter how old you are, everyone at every age has things to learn and things to move on from. Six years ago, you could not tell me that I would grow to be a woman who is actively trying to grow from the hurt and pain she has been through. I'm used to hiding my feelings and never having my voice heard about what is going on inside of me. It felt like the socially acceptable thing to do. The older I got, the more that I learned how important it is to express yourself and your feelings as much as you can. In doing that, I learned how to be myself which is turning into pure love for the person that I am becoming.

Confidence is a large part of the many things that we do. To even put together all of my thoughts in poetic form and create a book requires a certain level of confidence to believe that people will be interested in what I have to offer. I am in no way done with growing or learning all there is to know about this wonderful world and our unending universe. I believe that we never stop learning, but this has all been one important step closer to a full education. Socrates once said, "I am the wisest man alive, for I know one thing, and that is that I know nothing" and I let this teach me that just because I'm learning, doesn't mean I fully know.

Starting Over

I'm stronger than you play me for
So please don't disrespect me no more.
I gave my heart to you
And you acted like you didn't have a clue,
But I know you better than that.

Just because we didn't work
Doesn't mean I'm going to act
Like I have no self-worth.
It took me a lot of time to realize
That I can't even be mad at the shit you do
Because at the end of the day I am me
And you been you.

I'm still learning to love the girl I've become
'Cos I know I still have to grow,
But I'll be damned if you try to take that from me.

I lost parts of myself to you but now I plan on taking them
back.
No matter how much you try to act like you cared
When we all know we didn't,
Like you could love me
When we all know you couldn't.

I'm not a mad black woman, I'm a pissed black woman
So don't take my words lightly.
Just because I said all of that doesn't mean you should fear
the sight of me,
But that girl you played and took as a joke
Finally realized who she is, and I finally spoke.

No tears will fall from my eyes 'cos I refuse to cry.

You are too late.
My heart no longer weeps at the sound of your name.

I love you
So I never choose me.
You love me
So I never choose me.

You belittle me
But I still never choose me,
You call me names
But I still never choose me.

Now I realize choosing me
Will make me lose you.

The Return of Me

I feel strong today,
The type of strong that only happens because
I was the only one on my mind all day.

It makes my chest lighter,
My hair curlier,
My heart bigger.
The energy fills me,
The energy is me.

I don't ever wanna go
Back there again,
I don't ever want
My soul to disconnect from my spirit.

I don't ever want to feel
Like I shouldn't be me.

I don't ever want to forget
That my smile is as bright
As lanterns

Or that my skin is
As brown as cocoa beans
Or that my voice is a song.

I don't want to lean on
This week's lover
To tell me about me.

Now that I'm back, I hope
I never go anywhere else ever again.

Heartbreak Journey

First time around I was willing to pretend
That nothing ever happened, and if it did
It would never happen again.

Second time around I was slightly more aware.

Time and time again I was hurt.
To this day I consider my willingness to let new people in
A certain form of stupidity and naivety.
Yeah. Those are words that subconsciously describe me.

You're supposed to make the person you're with feel like the
only one in the world.
Not like they're in a competition with your lovers in the past.
You and those people are over and if you don't move on
then the good shit you have now won't last.

Yeah I may be insecure but the way you treat me and focus
on these other bitches wouldn't make anyone feel secure.

If you're not a cheater then you're a beater.
No, not with your hands but with your words.

With my mental health already swirling down the drain, you
would think that you could refrain
From this extreme emotional abuse.

I read my horoscope today.
It told me things will
Finally go my way.

I don't think my life
Works like that.

The planets seem to never align
And it feels as though
No one is ever on my side,
So should I even listen to it?

This positivity could
Fully flow through me

And I could be happy.

Let's see what happens.

Dreaming of You

Tell me something real.
Is it all just sex?
Simply a cheap thrill?

What goes on in your mind?
Do you think about what might be on mine?
Maybe you'll finally realize
That I think about you all the time.

I'm clueless and this is a mystery,
Whatever it is
Don't make our love history.

Truth is
I knew you'd leave again
But this time I said I wouldn't be lost
Or feel like I'm floating in the wind.

This is how most love stories begin.
I'll be the author of ours,
It helps keep my head out the stars
And my focus will be my own heart.

Woke up today
Feeling real different,
Nothing was gray.
I brush the bad thoughts off,
I don't want them to stay.

It's me who controls my mind,
No matter what I think,
It's not that disease that
Treats me so unkind.

Why have I been so blind?

I never knew my own potential
Or what made it so essential
To the person I wish to become.

I only hope with the new
Growth and clearance that she'll
Finally make an appearance

Because I've been waiting on her
For a long time.

PJ

Don't I amuse you?
I bet I confuse you.
Sights high, mind acres wide,
You can see the tips of mountains
And the depth of seas
In my eyes.

It's the ambition,
How's there's always a mission
That doesn't need to be for you to see.

Working towards learned self-worth,
Understanding what's deserved,
Still making all the mistakes.
What will it take?

Above it all, still enticing,
Even with all my problems deciding.

Chocolate toned, double-stacked
And a little sassy,

Therapeutic, real relaxed
And a little nasty.

Blessed ingredients,
A rare mix with a twist,
You can tell she knows who she is.

It's that healing glow,
The one gained with the power of saying no.

It's that self-love shine
While still being scared to let people inside.

Elemental, sometimes forgetful
But always classy.

In love with her and all,
Even the flaws I can't see.
I love her and she's me.

Love Letter

You hold anger right on the tip of your tongue
Ready to spit, spit it out at the first abuser.
You keep hate on your skin to
Remember what you can of your past.

You carry no love in your walk because you never had it.

But your tongue should be used to spew sweet words
And beautiful renditions of who you are.
Your brown skin should reflect the courage and bravery
That you put on every morning.

Your walk should be wide, sassy, and full of love
Because it is inside you.

Now find it.

Link

No matter how he puts it down,
It doesn't erase my crown.
I wanna believe these feelings of love
Are actually signs from above
But I really can't trust it.

Fuck it,
I'll try.
It'll probably make me cry
And have me asking myself "Why?"

People call you fake
And say you're a snake
But you only make me feel great.

Should I listen to advice
Or trust my feelings inside?

I'm tired of being conflicted
And I decided to not deal with all the pain
That you inflicted.

Not to mention this decision
Only causes me stress.
How am I to know what's best?

Maybe if I hurry and think fast
And do what I can to forget about the past.

I don't care what anybody thinks.
When do you wanna link?

With the rainy days
Come the fulfilling and good,
I try to look at the glass as
Half full.

Sunshine can't reach
Without the yearning,
Lessons can't teach
If you aren't open to new learning.

Even when crashing down
I find my way,
Positivity lives in those sun rays.

I'm bursting out
To never go back in,
The freedom is no longer spreading me thin.
I'm a brand new woman

And finally loving this skin.

I believe in true love,
That's how I know you aren't the one.

I want the one that
Makes it hard to breathe,
Makes me realize I can't see,
I want them to need
Every part of me.

I want to make them my home,
Be with them and forget I have a phone,
I want someone that's mine.
I hate not acting on lingering temptations.
I feel like my fate is waiting,

My true heart's desire
Never fading.
The passion expels from me but it's on me in my vision,
I chase the ones that avoid me with precision.

My head is in the clouds
Thinking about the only one
Who isn't around.
Maybe I'm a fool

Because I cannot choose?
Because he will have my heart no matter what I do.
That's the truth.

So I don't mean to be your heart breaker.
I did not know you could never be this heart's taker.
If I didn't believe in love,
If I didn't believe he could
Still give me the sun,

Then maybe you could be the one.
Exhaustion clouds my brain,
It feels like I have no emotion,
I only feel drained.

All thoughts are fragmented
And the fragments are sharp,
I act like they don't exist
So it doesn't reach my heart.

I pull them all out for my art.
Other than that I keep it in
So I don't fall apart.

I'm way too preoccupied
With finding someone to be by my side,
Never made the consideration
That all the sexual temptation
Would be my downfall.

I'm starting to regret it all.

I let passing infatuation
Constantly leave a permanent indentation.

I let complicated situations
Make me forget that life should be a celebration.

Eventually I see I'm on the hook,
There's nothing left to do but open this book
And I let it all out.

I take the pages and read about a better me
Because that is what the journey is all about.
My brain is still cloudy
And my feelings are rowdy,

But I know I'm ready for a new day.

Life is complicated,
It's filled with lights that burn out
Unexpectedly
And can never be turned on again.

How do I reminisce without longing?
At least the last time was nice.
I should've given you your love back then
Because I knew it was the end.

I feel like I'm losing myself,
Black queen with thick hips
And quick wits,
As soon as it goes south, she dips.

Now I linger,
No longer a lead singer,
Willing to be the background
As long as all that love I lost is found.

Who is that?
That doesn't fight back?
Willing to be the victim of every attack
Just because they said they loved her back.

I don't wanna be her
But I want to be her friend
So that she knows it's okay
To start over again.

Reevaluation

A joke
Making me feel like I wish
We never even spoke.

I lost my way,
That leaves a person with nothing else to say.
I have a tendency to be blind,
I lose my mind and my heart crosses a line.

I feel angry
But the only person to blame is me,
The red flags in the wind,
The targets on my heart,
I took none of that as a warning.
If I did it would've been over from the start.

I ask myself all these questions
Because I never learn my lesson.
I'm tired of failing every test.
The empty conversations are finally starting
To reveal what's next.

I have all of these feelings
I thought it was safe to release
But I don't know what I was thinking,

It sounded too sweet.

I'm thinking it all over.
What's all this pain really for?
I need to learn when to close the door.
Wearing my heart on my sleeve
Is having its consequences.
That's fine though and
I hope I feel healed when I'm reminiscing.

Here's to reevaluation and empty wishing.

Emily

Respect me none and love me scarcely
So that I may know true desire.
Decadent when in the mood
But the emotions are always haunting.

Mysterious in nature,
Beautiful by choice,
I always need them wanting
Guidance in my pen,
My book's journey beside me.
My descent is truly daunting.

Talks With the Moon

Bad thoughts funnel into my brain,
Erasing everything with no peace to remain.

Late and long nights with the moon,
The light illuminating all my flaws.
Even through the darkness I still swoon.

Our conversations are complicated
But when I see her I'm still elated.

We read together,
Bleed together,
It's a tie that can never be severed.

She pushed me inspiration when I'm grasping at straws due
to desperation,
She reminds me who I am when I let someone tear me
down again,

When it's full
I feel a different kind of pull,

Logic is lost,
All actions are done with no thought of a cost.
Every time I start my story I hesitate,

She brings out all my feelings of self-hate
But I forgive her every time.

I'm still the saddest to see her go
When the sun starts to show.

Patiently and anxiously, I await every night
Hoping this time everything will go right.

Wintertime Bliss

Swept up in emotions,
Ready to give all my devotion
Just for this winter land romance.
I didn't know that
We never stood a chance.

Chocolate candied kisses,
Sugar coated promises,
I loved the way you made me feel
And the things you helped me forget.

Constantly thinking and worrying
That it was all too good to be true,
Tried to convince myself that I had to adjust to it
Because it's new.

I'm learning that it's really not good to ignore
All the things you've noticed aren't healthy before.
Never again will I be ruled by my attraction
Especially to someone who doesn't want to stick around
And is just a distraction.

I now have to remember your touch as ice cold,
And forget all the sweet things that I've been told,
But when I'm freezing I'll sit and reminisce
About our wintertime bliss.

Self-Love

Your skin is glowing,
How do you master it?
You're really a beauty,
Can I capture it?

A treasure to behold,
One I want to give my life,

I'm in the mirror,
Smitten,
No longer worried about
How I fit in.

On a path,
A Journey,
And behind every corner there's
Lurking

My insecurities,
All the bullies,
But I won't let that get to me.

I have been awakened,
The Goddess,
They'll realize they made a mistake and

It'll no longer concern me

Because I am finally free.